THE G.I. SERIES

The Big Red One

A 1st Infantry Division Jeep is driven ashore from a Landing Craft, Vehicle, Personnel (LCVP). After the North African landings the wooden LCVP, otherwise known as the Higgins Boat after its inventor and principal builder Andrew Higgins, was a mainstay of Allied amphibious assaults. It could carry 36 men or a 3-ton vehicle directly on to a beach. (SC152175

THE G.I. SERIES

THE ILLUSTRATED HISTORY OF THE AMERICAN
SOLDIER, HIS UNIFORM AND HIS EQUIPMENT

The Big Red One

THE 1ST INFANTRY DIVISION, 1917–1970

Christopher J. Anderson

Greenhill Books
LONDON
Stackpole Books
PENNSYLVANIA

Greenhill Books

This book is dedicated to Dawn Gould, who
still remembers her GIs

The Big Red One
first published 2003 by Greenhill Books, Lionel
Leventhal Limited, Park House, 1 Russell Gardens,
London NW11 9NN
www.greenhillbooks.com
and
Stackpole Books, 5067 Ritter Road, Mechanicsburg,
PA 17055, U.S.A.

British Library Cataloguing in Publication Data
Anderson, Christopher J.
The Big Red One. - (The G.I. Series: the illustrated
history of the American soldier, his uniform and his
equipment; v.31)
1. United States. Army. Infantry Division, 1st - History
2. United States. Army. Infantry Division, 1st -
Equipment
3. United States. Army. Infantry Division, 1st -
Uniforms
I. Title
356.1'0973

ISBN 1-85367-528-8

Library of Congress Cataloging-in-Publication Data
available

All photographs are courtesy of the U.S. National
Archives unless otherwise noted.

Designed by David Gibbons, DAG Publications Ltd
Layout by Anthony A. Evans, DAG Publications Ltd
Printed in China

THE BIG RED ONE
THE 1ST INFANTRY DIVISION, 1917–1970

In the spring of 1917, while Europe's major powers were locked in a gigantic struggle involving millions of men, the minuscule United States Army was scattered across America in a variety of tiny posts, and still organized in much the same way that it had been when it was engaged in fighting the Plains Indians. All of that changed abruptly on April 6, 1917, when President Woodrow Wilson declared war on Imperial Germany and its Allies. After staying out of "Europe's War" for almost three years, America was going to send her sons to fight.

While it may have been an easy thing to deliver the speech that brought American into a world war, it was quite another to prepare an Army that would be able to fight it. Aside from a brief military expedition into Mexico in 1916 to chase the outlaw Pancho Villa, the Army had seen no major military operation since the Philippine insurrection at the end of the nineteenth century. While well-organized and highly structured European armies were fighting complex battles involving divisions, corps and armies, the largest permanent U.S. Army formation in 1917 was the regiment.

Army leaders were aware that it was not only necessary to recruit thousands of men, but it was also necessary to prepare the materiel and organization required of a global war. The Allies, however, had little time to wait for the Americans to make all of the necessary preparations before entering the fray. General John J. "Black Jack" Pershing was to command the American Expeditionary Force (AEF), the American army that would be sent to France. In a gesture of support and in order to get into the fight as quickly as possible, the Army organized existing Regular Army and National Guard units into larger divisions that could be quickly sent to France. On May 24, 1917, the first of these units, the 1st Expeditionary Division, was ordered constituted from existing Regular Army units.

The new division benefited by having some of the oldest and most distinguished regiments in the Army assigned to it. The 1st Brigade consisted of the 16th and 18th Infantry Regiments, the 2nd was assigned the 26th and 28th Infantry Regiments. The 5th, 6th and 7th Field Artillery Regiments provided the artillery support. Specialist troops such as engineers, signals, etc., came from various other Regular Army units. Brig. Gen. William L. Sibert commanded the new unit. When organization had been completed, the division was transported to France in June 1917.

A week after their arrival, on July 4, 1917, the 16th Infantry's 2nd Battalion represented the division in a parade through the streets of Paris. One of the division's staff officers remarked to a French delegation sent to greet the Americans, "Lafayette, we are here!" Two days later the division was redesignated as the 1st Division.

Throughout that summer, French and British instructors—veterans of trench warfare—worked with the untried Americans to prepare them for what they were about to face and at 06:05 a.m. on October 23, Battery C of the 6th Field Artillery fired the first American shell of the war against the Germans. In December, General Sibert was recalled to Washington; he was replaced by Maj. Gen. Robert Bullard. It was Bullard who would lead the division during its first great test.

Desperate to secure victory before the full weight of American might could be felt, in the spring of 1918 the Germans launched their *Kaiserschlacht* offensive against weary French and British units in Picardy. Beginning on March 21, German units crashed through Allied lines and made advances on a scale not seen since the earliest days of the war. Soon, they were again threatening Paris. Believing that they faced defeat, the French appealed to Pershing for troops. The AEF commander agreed, but maintained his long running demand that, once the enemy offensive had been stopped, his men go in to combat in their own formations. The French, reluctantly, agreed to a compromise: if the Americans demonstrated their ability in their first action, then they would no longer demand that the AEF be broken up and its men parceled out as replacements to Allied units.

That first test would come at Cantigny, a tiny town that the French had been unable to retake from the Germans. On May 28, 1918, just over a year after America had declared war, the 1st Division's 28th Infantry left their trenches and attacked the town. Cantigny was secured in just 45 minutes and held for several days despite repeated German counterattacks. The 28th Infantry—known forever afterward as the "Lions of Cantigny"—had demonstrated that the AEF was capable of holding its own against the best the Germans could throw at them. After Cantigny, there was no longer any discussion of splitting up the AEF.

Just days after this victory, the 28th Infantry and the rest of the division were sent to the Soissons sector. Along with the 2nd Infantry Division and the French 1st Moroccan Division, the 1st had been selected to lead Field

Marshal Ferdinand Foch's counterattack in the region. Early on the morning of July 18, the attack began. By 08:00 a.m. the division had advanced a mile into the German defenses. By the 22nd, the three divisions had cut the Château-Thierry road and forced the Germans to retreat from the town of Soissons. The 1st Division had suffered more than 7,000 casualties during the offensive.

In September the division participated in the Saint Mihiel offensive. It was the U.S. First Army's first major operation. The attack began on September 11 and by the 13th the division, advancing northward, met the 26th Infantry Division at Hattonchatel and closed the salient. With little time to rest, the 1st was then assigned to take part in the Meuse-Argonne offensive, where it was involved in the brutal fighting until November.

At 11:00 a.m. on November 11, 1918, when the guns finally fell silent, the division was in positions overlooking Sedan. In its 223 days on the line, the 1st had earned a reputation as among the most formidable American units. Five members of the division were awarded the Medal of Honor and its flags were decorated with six campaign streamers. Such a reputation, however, had come at a heavy price. The division suffered more than 22,000 casualties during the war—the second highest casualty rate of any American division.

In recognition of this performance, the 1st was selected to serve on occupation duty in Germany. The division crossed the Rhine in November 1918 and remained in Germany until September of the following year. After their return to the States, the division's units were separated and assigned to posts along the East Coast.

The 1st spent the two decades between the wars in garrison duties and peacetime routine. With America in the grip of the Great Depression, little effort was made to bring the division's separate units together to train and prepare for another war. It was not until 1939, with Europe embarking on its second world war, that the Army began to make the changes necessary for its units to fight a more modern, mechanized, conflict. For the 1st, it meant that the division was "triangularized," with three infantry and four artillery regiments. In June 1940, the 28th Infantry was reassigned to the 8th Infantry Division and the 32nd and 33rd Field Artillery regiments—formed in part from the old 6th Artillery Regiment—became part of the division.

The division's separate units came together again in 1940 to take part in the Louisiana Maneuvers. Prophetically, a year later the division was in New River, North Carolina, to take part in amphibious maneuvers with the 1st Marine Division. Both units would soon be involved in some of the most famous amphibious assaults in military history. The 1st was at Fort Devens, Mass., on December 7, 1941, when the Japanese attacked Pearl Harbor and brought America into World War II.

In June 1942, after further maneuvers, the division was alerted for overseas movement and in August the men boarded the *Queen Mary* and sailed for England. After arrival in Great Britain, Maj. Gen., Terry de la Mesa Allen, the division commander, kept his men busy preparing for their first operation of the war, Operation Torch.

In September, the division left Tidworth Barracks, near Salisbury, where it had been stationed and boarded SS *Reina del Pacifico* bound for Algeria. Despite unexpected resistance from Vichy French forces, the 1st's landings at Arzew and Les Andalouses went well and by November 10 Oran had been secured. For the remainder of the year the division's regiments, either operating separately or with French and British units, became acclimatized to combat conditions and continued the piecemeal advance across Algeria and into Tunisia.

On February 14, 1943, Field Marshal Erwin Rommel launched an attack against the U.S. II Corps. He hoped to deliver a resounding defeat to the inexperienced American forces to shatter their morale and to try and restore the initiative in Tunisia. At first, it seemed that his attack would succeed. The 21st Panzer Division brushed aside the 1st Armored Division as well as elements of the 1st Infantry Division. Eventually, however, the attack was halted and a month later, on March 17, the 1st Infantry launched counterattacks at Gafsa and El Guettar that retook much of the ground lost in February.

American advances continued and by April the Allies were fighting their final battles in North Africa. On May 7, the same day that the *Afrika Korps* surrendered, the division was relieved in preparation for its next assignment—Operation Husky, the invasion of Sicily. While it had suffered some setbacks during the campaign, most notably at Kasserine, the 1st had benefited greatly from its campaign in North Africa and learned valuable lessons about modern combat.

The division's 16th and 26th Infantry landed at Gela, Sicily, on July 10. Although the Italians put up little opposition to the landings, the Germans reacted by quickly sending the elite *Hermann Göring* Panzer Division to wipe out the beachhead. In one of the most tenacious actions of the war, the 1st, along with elements of the 82nd Airborne, stopped repeated German armored attacks on the beachhead. Lieutenant General Omar Bradley later commented that he did not know if there was any other division that would have held its ground under similar circumstances. "Only the perverse Big Red One with its no less perverse commander was both hard and experienced enough to take that assault in stride."

After securing the beach, the division moved inland, fighting through strong German defenses along the Allies' western axis of advance. On July 17 the division took Enna, the capital city. Nicosia fell ten days later and on August 6, after it had fended off two dozen German counterattacks, it took Troina. The 37 days of almost continuous combat had cost the 1st more than 250 men killed and another 1,100 wounded. It had also earned the enmity of senior American commanders who believed that Allen and the men of the 1st were just a bit too sure of themselves. On August 7, Allen, and his assistant division commander, Brig. Gen. Theodore Roosevelt, were relieved. Maj. Gen. Clarence R. Huebner, a veteran soldier who had begun his military career as an enlisted man in the 16th Infantry in 1910, replaced Allen.

Back in England by November 1943, the 1st began training for what would be considered its most important mission, the invasion of France. By 1944, there were few other divisions in the Army that could claim to have as much amphibious warfare experience as the 1st Infantry Division. For this reason, the Big Red One was given one of the most difficult missions of the entire D-Day landings. The 1st's 16th Infantry Regiment (with elements of the 29th Infantry Division's 116th Infantry Regiment attached) would land and secure a beach, code-named Omaha, between Colleville-sur-Mer and Vierville-sur-Mer and then move inland with the rest of the V Corps toward Caumont and St. Lô.

At 06:30 a.m. on June 6, 1944, the ramps of the landing craft went down on Omaha Beach and the men of the 2nd Battalion, 16th Infantry Regiment walked into a maelstrom. German defenders from the 726th Infantry Regiment, firing from positions that had received little damage from pre-invasion barrages, devastated the troops who landed. The battalion was quickly pinned down and subsequent waves landing behind fared little better. So bad was the situation that General Bradley even considered diverting reinforcements to other beaches. As the morning wore on, however, small groups of men began to advance despite the enemy fire. Colonel George A. Taylor, the 16th Infantry's commander, yelled at those around him, "Two kinds of people are staying on this beach, the dead and those who are going to die. Now let's get the hell out of here!" By mid-morning, more and more men had mustered the courage necessary to cover the open ground and move inland. At 1:30 p.m. Bradley received word that the troops on Omaha were moving inland. It had been a near run thing.

Bradley later commented, "Had a less experienced division than the 1st Infantry stumbled into this crack resistance, it might easily have been thrown back into the Channel. Unjust though it was, my choice of the 1st to spearhead the invasion probably saved us Omaha Beach and a catastrophe on the landing." The losses, however, had been appalling. The division suffered more than 3,000 casualties, a thousand of which were suffered in the 16th Infantry Regiment alone.

Along with the rest of the First Army, the 1st Division then participated in the grueling fighting in the Norman *bocage.* The division remained on the line until July 14, 1944, when the 5th Infantry Division relieved it. After a few days to rest and refit, the 1st was then reassigned to the VII Corps to participate in the breakout from St. Lô to cut off the Germans trapped in Brittany and destroy the remnants of the Seventh German Army. After the slow progress of June and July, August was a month of lightning advances as the Allies liberated large portions of France. Moving an average of 20 miles a day, the last week of the month saw the division cross more than 300 miles of territory, ending on the 31st at Soissons, where the division had fought with such distinction during World War I. September found the division entering Belgium. After liberating Liège it was on to the German Siegfried Line and the German border, which was reached on September 12 and Aachen, Germany, was soon under attack.

As the first major city in Germany to be threatened with capture by the Allies, Adolf Hitler had ordered the defenders of Aachen to hold the city until the very end. And they almost did. In some of the most brutal fighting of the war, the 1st Division, along with other U.S. divisions, battled the Germans through September and into October. It was not until the 21st that the city finally surrendered.

From the rubble of Aachen the 1st was then ordered south to advance through the Hürtgen Forrest and cross the Roer River. Attacks through November to take the Gressenich Woods, Heistern and other tiny towns cost the division thousands of casualties for little or no strategic gain. Fighting continued until December 7, 1944, when the division was finally relieved and sent to the Ardennes where it was to be allowed to rest and refit.

It was not until December 14 that all of the division's units had been able to extricate themselves from the Hürtgen and gather around Henri-Chapelle, Belgium. The division's officers barely had time to learn what their new commander, Maj. Gen. Clifton Andrus, expected, and weary veterans and anxious recruits had had little time to acquaint themselves with one another, when, two days later, at 05:00 a.m., the Germans launched their massive Ardennes offensive. Designed to split the American and British armies and re-take the vital port city of Antwerp, Hitler's offensive made rapid progress. The 1st was in the area north of Eupen and was quickly brought into the battle along the northern shoulder of the German breakthrough around Butgenbach. After rounding up members of August von der Heydte's badly conducted parachute drop, the division was busy slowing down various German armored formations.

When the Germans were no longer able to advance, the 1st was one of the units that quickly counterattacked. It remained on the offensive until January 30, when the 1st again reached the German border. The fighting in the Ardennes had cost the division an additional 2,000 casualties. On February 25 the Roer River was crossed and the advance continued. The 1st fought and took Bonn, Germany, on March 8 and crossed the Rhine on the 16th.

Through March and April the division advanced across Germany. Sometimes resistance was light; at other times German soldiers defended their positions resolutely. On April 1, 1945, the 1st made its longest tactical advance of the war, moving more than 150 miles through enemy territory in a single day. A week later, the division crossed the Weser River into Czechoslovakia, where it was on May 8, 1945, when the war in Europe finally came to an end.

In 443 days of combat the division had suffered some 20,000 casualties among the 43,743 men to serve in its ranks. As evidence of its accomplishments, division members earned countless personal awards, including 16 Medals of Honor, and the 1st had been recognized with eight campaign streamers, two French *Croix de Guerres* with palms, the *Fourragère* to the *Croix de Guerre* and the Belgian *Fourragère.* Perhaps more importantly, the 1st was recognized by friend and foe alike as among the most accomplished American divisions of the war. As one German officer commented, "Where the 1st Division was, there we would have trouble."

While thousands of men were demobilized and numerous divisions returned home, the 1st Division remained in Germany after the war to take up its familiar mission of occupation duty. During the Korean War it was stationed along the eastern border of West Germany, prepared to defend the cuntry against a Russian invasion if necessary. It remained in Germany until the spring of 1955, when it returned to the U.S. and set up its headquarters at Fort Riley, Kansas. It was the first time the division's colors had been home in 13 years.

For the next ten years the division remained at Fort Riley where it trained for its next assignment. The call came in April 1965 when, as part of the larger build up of U.S. forces in the Republic of (South) Vietnam, the division received word that it should make preparations for deployment overseas. On June 23, 1965, PFC Gerard Werster of the 7th Artillery Regiment came ashore at Qui Nhon, Republic of Vietnam. Over the course of the next several months, Werster would be joined by thousands of other members of the Big Red One, which was the first divisional-sized unit deployed to Vietnam.

The 28th Infantry Regiment had rejoined the division prior to Vietnam. The 1st was further augmented by the 2nd Infantry Regiment and aviation and armored assets.

Elements of the division came under fire for the first time at 00:17 a.m. on July 17, 1965, near Bien Hoa, north of Saigon, where the 1st would establish its home base. It was the beginning of the division's longest war.

On July 22, 1965, Company B, 2nd Battalion, 16th Infantry, conducted a search and destroy operation in the vicinity of the Bien Hoa base camp. Meanwhile, the remainder of the division continued its deployment. The whole division, under the command of Maj. Gen. Jonathan O. Seaman, was declared operational on November 1, 1965. The remainder of the year was spent in small-scale operations near Bien Hoa to secure the area around the division's base camp. With the division finally assembled, 1966 saw an increase in the tempo of operations. In March, Seaman was replaced by Brig. Gen. William E. DePuy, who developed a number of tactical innovations that improved his division's performance against the enemy. By April the 1st was involved in Tay Ninh Province in Operation Birmingham, which was followed by Operation El Paso in May. During the summer, the division fought a series of battles to keep Highway 13 open and in August the 2nd Infantry engaged and destroyed a Vietcong battalion at the Battle of Bong Trang. In November the entire division was involved against the 9th VC Division in Operation Attleboro.

The next year saw the division move into the Iron Triangle for Operation Cedar Falls and on February 22, 1967, after replacing DePuy, Maj. Gen. John H. Hay led the division in Operation Junction City, which was the largest operation of the war up to that point. At Ap Gu on April 1, elements of the 16th and 26th Infantry repulsed repeated Communist human wave assaults that left more than 600 enemy dead.

The men of the Big Red One continued their operations around Saigon through 1967. In late January 1968, at the start of the North Vietnamese Tet Offensive, the division became heavily engaged in the battles fought around Saigon. During the two weeks of the enemy offensive, the division was credited with inflicting more than 1,500 casualties on the enemy. In March, Maj. Gen. Keith Ware, a Medal of Honor recipient, replaced General Hay. The rest of the year was spent eliminating remaining enemy formations in and around Saigon and in August elements of the 2nd Infantry Regiment helped relieve the Special Forces base at Loc Ninh.

On September 14, Maj. Gen. Orwin C. Talbott took command of the division. Talbott led the 1st in its continued operations around Saigon and, in the summer of 1969, began working to help prepare the South Vietnamese Army to take on a bigger role in its nation's defense. In August, Talbott was replaced by Maj. Gen.

Albert E. Milloy, who led the division during renewed battles around Saigon and to defend Highway 13.

At the end of 1969, Milloy received word that he should start preparing his division to return to the United States. By April 1970 the entire division was back at Fort Riley, Kansas. Despite the confusion and disappointment of Vietnam, the division had performed admirably. By the time of its departure in 1970, the division's area of responsibility north of Saigon was essentially devoid of Communist activity. In April, as the division prepared to depart, Milloy remarked, "We have worked ourselves out of a job."

During its 1,656 days in Vietnam the division had suffered more than 20,000 casualties, more than it had suffered during World War II. Its flag was decorated with a further 11 campaign streamers and numerous Vietnamese awards. Eleven members of the division were decorated with the Medal of Honor.

With its redeployment to Fort Riley, the 1st began one of its most profound conversions. Beginning that year, the most distinguished infantry unit in the United States Army was reorganized as a mechanized division. It continues to serve in that capacity today.

In July 1944, during a ceremony to recognize their heroism on Omaha Beach, Supreme Commander Dwight D. Eisenhower addressed the members of the Big Red One: "I know your record from the day you landed in Africa, then Sicily. I am beginning to think that the 1st Division is a sort of Praetorian Guard." Eisenhower was not too far off the mark. Since its founding in 1917, the 1st Division has always been at the forefront of American military operations and is regularly called on to live up to its motto, "No Mission too Difficult, No Sacrifice too Great, Duty First!"

FURTHER READING

The Society of the First Division, *History of the First Division During the World War 1917-1918*, 1919

Hays Outoupalik, Dennis Gordon, Paul Schulz, *World War One Collector's Handbook*, 1979

Laurence Stallings, *The Doughboys: The Story of the AEF in World War I*, 1963

Jonathan Gawne, *Over There: The American Soldier in World War I*, 1997

Kenneth Lewis, *Doughboy to GI: U.S. Army Clothing and Equipment 1900-1945*, 1998

Society of the First Division, *Danger Forward: The Story of the First Division in World War II*, 1946

Ian V. Hogg, ed., *The American Arsenal: World War II Official Standard Ordnance Catalog*, 2001

Philip Katcher, *US 1st Infantry Division 1939-1945*, 1978

Richard Windrow and Tim Hawkins, *The World War II GI: US Army Uniforms 1941-1945*, 1999

Jonathan Gawne, *Spearheading D-Day*, 1998

Shelby Stanton, *World War II Order of Battle*, 1984

Jonathan Gawne, *U.S. Army Photo Album: Shooting the War in Color, 1941-1945 USA to ETO*, 1996

Kevin Lyles, *Vietnam: US Uniforms in Colour Photographs*, 1993

Leroy Thompson, *The U.S. Army in Vietnam*, 1990

Shelby Stanton, *U.S. Army Uniforms of the Vietnam War*, 1992

Shelby Stanton, *Vietnam Order of Battle*, 1981

Right: William Aylward's *American Troops' Supply Train* depicts a convoy moving men and equipment to the front. The first American war of the 20th century found the members of the 1st Infantry Division, and the other units of the American Expeditionary Force, heavily reliant on horse drawn transport. (CC38891)

Right: Harvey Dunn's *A Painting of World War I*, shows an American "Liberty Truck" moving men and equipment to the front. The officers in the painting are wearing trench coats like those worn by British officers. Among the first American troops to arrive in France, the officers and men of the 1st adopted many uniform items inspired by their French and British allies. (CC38894)

Right: In another WWI scene painted by Dunn, GIs advance through barbed wire defenses behind French-built Renault tanks. The men are equipped with M1903 Springfield rifles. The 1st Division's troops were equipped with this weapon but the most common U.S. service rifle of the war was the P17 Enfield. (CC38895)

Above left: A 1st Division 2½ ton truck is loaded on to a Landing Ship, Tank (LST) prior to the invasion of France. The truck has been nicknamed "SNAFU," which was painted in yellow gas-detection paint on the front edge of the hood. Men from a variety of services are clustered around the LST, but an officer from the 1st Division (center foreground in sun glasses) can be seen overseeing the loading. He has been able to obtain a pair of the highly coveted paratrooper jump boots. (CC1247)

Above right: One of the most famous images of the war shows members of the 1st Division about to be transported to the invasion beaches in France. The men are wearing a mixture of winter combat jackets—better known as "tanker jackets"—and Parson's Field Jackets—better known among collectors as M41 field jackets. Since the Army was racially segregated in 1944, the African-American serviceman shown at the right of the picture cannot have been a 1st Division member but may have been from one of the Navy's many Engineer Special Brigades that supported the invasion. (CC1258)

Left: Artillerymen from the 32nd Field Artillery wait along an English road en route to the marshaling areas. The C9 on the back of the truck identifies this truck as the ninth vehicle of Battery C. The majority of the men in the picture are wearing herringbone twill (HBT) cotton uniforms that have, most likely, been impregnated with anti-gas treatment.

Above, left: Private Clyde Peacock, a 1st Division MP, waits to board his transport craft. Although he does not have divisional insignia on his jacket, Peacock's helmet is stenciled with the "Big Red One." The yellow MP letters painted on the helmet indicate his assignment to a divisional level military police unit. He has been able to acquire a pair of leather gloves. (CC1228)

Above, right: A 1st Division Jeep is loaded onto its transport. Each infantry division was allocated 612 of the versatile ¼-ton Jeeps. This Jeep is assigned to Battery F of the division's 32nd Field Artillery Battalion, which can be seen painted on the Jeep's bumper. Like the other vehicles used in the invasion, the Jeeps were specially fitted out with various equipment that allowed them to be driven from their transports through the surf and on to the beach. One of these was a snorkel, which can be seen supported on the right side of the windshield, this allowed air to reach the engine. (CC001092)

Left: Members of the 1st rest around their Jeeps aboard a landing craft prior to departing for France. Most of the men are wearing life preservers around their waists. These floatation devices could be instantly inflated by activating the two CO_2 cartridges located at the front of the belt. During the invasion it was found, however, that when the belts were inflated, they frequently caused the wearers to lose their balance and flip over in the water. (CC1273)

Above: Corporal Michael Penzilik enjoys mail from home, "somewhere in Germany." Penzilik is wearing an early pair of HBT fatigues in the distinctive light pea-green shade. He is resting under a two-man shelter tent. Each GI was equipped with a half of one of these tents and would snap his half together with his partner's to form a small tent. Penzilik is using a wooden box that he has engraved with the divisional insignia as a writing desk. (CC1132)

Above right: Major General Clarence R. Huebner became the division commander after Major General Terry Allen was relieved of command in July 1943. Huebner commanded the division from July 1943 until his promotion to corps command in December 1944. He had begun his service in the Army as a private in the 16th Infantry Regiment. Huebner is wearing the popular tanker's jacket over his wool uniform. Slung over his shoulder is a .45-caliber pistol. Huebner is standing amidst recently captured Siegfried Line fortifications. (CC2309)

Left: Members of the 1st Infantry Division's 18th Infantry Regiment stand guard over the defendants at the Nuremberg war crimes trial early in 1946. The men are all wearing the wool service coat. Originally designed as a combat garment, the service coat was used throughout the war as a dress uniform. The 18th Infantry's distinctive insignia (DI) can be seen on the lapels of the coats. The guards used the white helmet liners and web belts during the trial. (CCETO3702)

Right: Maj. Gen. Harry C. Ingles, Chief Signal Corps Officer during World War II (left), is seated next to his son John, a first lieutenant in the 1st Infantry Division. Both men are wearing the tropical worsted wool summer service uniform. John wears his branch insignia (in this case crossed cannon) on the lapel of his jacket. His units DIs are worn on the epaulettes of his jacket, above his rank insignia. (CC3438)

Right: Soldiers of the 1st Battalion, 18th Infantry Regiment, are trucked to Bien Hoa airbase after landing at Cam Rahn Bay on July 12, 1965. The 1st was the first U.S. Army division to be deployed to Vietnam. These men are all wearing Olive Green (OG) 107 cotton utility uniforms. They are armed with M14 rifles, which had replaced the M1 Garand rifles that had been used during World War II and Korea. (CC31471)

Right: Sergeant Jerome Mock (left) and PFC David Smith from the 16th Infantry Regiment test an AN-PPS-4 radar set at the division's Bien Hoa base camp in August 1965. Advanced radar equipment like the PPS-4 was intended to detect enemy infiltrators. While Mock wears the OG107 utility uniform, Smith has been able to obtain a set of the tropical combat uniform, more widely known as the jungle jacket and trousers. (CC31573)

Left: A member of Company C, 16th Infantry Regiment, crouches in some tall grass while reloading his M14 during a patrol in October 1965. The photograph provides a good illustration of the camouflage helmet cover for the M1 helmet. The cover, inspired by the Marine Corps' camouflage covers of WWII, was reversible, with green colors, intended for use during spring and summer on one side, and brown for fall and winter on the other. The green side was generally left showing in Vietnam. (CC32312)

Left: Second Lieutenant John L. Libs, Company C, 16th Infantry Regiment, reports on the situation during a patrol. Sergeant Ralph Vogueli, the assistant platoon sergeant, is to Libs' right. The lieutenant is speaking into the handset of a PRC-25 radio, which could send a signal up to 3 kilometers. A full-color version of the divisional insignia can be seen on Libs' left shoulder. (CC32313)

Left: Men from Battery C, 32nd Field Artillery, question a suspected communist guerrilla during a mission near Cu Chi in January 1966. The soldier seated at right is wearing a locally manufactured camouflage bush hat. These hats were privately purchased from Vietnamese vendors and were very popular with GIs. He is also wearing the black leather combat boot, which was eventually replaced with the leather and nylon jungle boot. (CC33259)

Above: Platoon Sergeant Arnold Owens from Battery A, 33rd Field Artillery, directs fire from a stack of ammunition boxes during Operation Attleboro II in November 1966. Rounds for Owens' 105mm howitzer are packaged in the brown cardboard tubes stacked behind the gun. The 105 was a lightweight artillery piece that could hit targets out to 7 miles. (CC37483)

Above: PFC Milt D. Longstaff searches a Viet Cong tunnel in the Iron Triangle with his M2A7 portable flamethrower at the ready. The 42-pound weapon was ideal for clearing enemy positions, but its distinctive fuel tanks made the operator a tempting target for enemy soldiers. (CC37982)

Right: Sergeant H. Wakeguchi has taped two clips for his M14 rifle together with green tape. Each of the clips held 20 rounds of 7.62mm ammunition. Additional rounds would be carried in the ammunition pouches of the M195LCE (Load Carrying Equipment) or bandoliers. (CC32302)

Right: During Operation Cedar Falls members of HQ Company, 28th Infantry Regiment, guide a CH-47 helicopter in to a recently cleared landing zone. The radio telephone operator (RTO) has a hands-free headset over his helmet while his officer talks to the helicopter with the handset of the PRC-25 radio. The handset has been wrapped in plastic to protect it from moisture. (CC37989)

Right: Members of the 1st Division climb aboard an M113A1 Armored Personnel Carrier (APC). This APC has been fitted with an "Okinawa" shield to protect the operator of the .50-caliber machine gun. The vehicle-mounted .50-caliber M2 provided additional firepower that could support the infantrymen once they had disembarked from the vehicle. (CC38083)

Right: PFC Walton Clark, an RTO with the Recon Platoon of the 28th Infantry Regiment, during Operation Billings. Clark is wearing a locally manufactured bush hat and jungle fatigues. The handset for his radio can be seen clipped to the right side of his LCE harness. He carries seven clips for his M16 rifle in an M193 cotton bandolier.

Above: Doughboys train with *Poilus* from the 47th Chasseur Division. The 47th was stationed near the 1st Division at Gondrecourt and was responsible for familiarizing the Americans with the conditions they would encounter on the front lines. The doughboys, in felt campaign hats, are being instructed on a variety of French weapons, including the Chauchat light machine gun. The 8mm Chauchat was eventually issued to 23 American divisions, including the 1st, because the U.S. Army lacked a light machine gun of its own manufacture. Before the war's end, the government had purchased 29,000 of the weapons from their French allies. (SC687)

Below: Members of the 1st rest in a village during a road march after their arrival in France in the summer of 1917. These men are dressed as they would have been during the 1916 punitive expedition to Mexico. They are all wearing the campaign hat with wool breeches and shirts. Rather than leggings, which would soon become standard issue, these men are still wearing canvas leggings. (SC688)

Left: GIs from the 1st play with French children prior to going to the front. These men are all wearing campaign hats with silk branch of service hat cords. The branch color for infantry was light blue. The photograph illustrates the variety of ways that the men would personalize their campaign hats. (SC684)

Center left: Members of the division train with French M2 gas masks, which were issued to the division on its arrival in France because the Army was unable to supply American-made masks. Although most American troops eventually received British—and later American—box respirators, the M2 was retained as a reserve gas mask until the end of the war. (SC3127)

Bottom left: 1st Division artillerymen work on their newly issued French 75mm field pieces. The division's 6th and 7th Field Artillery Regiments were issued with the 75mm and designated as "light" field artillery regiments. A state-of-the-art recoil system allowed the gun to be fired up to ranges of 5½ miles without having to re-sight the gun after every shot. This allowed the 75 to be fired at rates far greater than any comparable German weapon. (3203)

Right: Artillerymen receive orders for their battery through field telephones. Two of the men are wearing leather leggings, which were better suited to working with horses and their associated tack and equipment. While they were easy to use, the landlines between field phones were easily severed during combat and going out to repair severed communications lines became a common chore for the doughboys. (SC3207)

Center right: A crew works their 75mm. So rapid was the gun's rate of fire that these men have set up their limber right next to the gun. When the gun completed its recoil, the man seated at right would pull the handle at the breech, which would eject the shell and allow the soldier at the trail to seat another round. (SC3210)

Below: The staff of the 1st Division at Gondrecourt, France. Maj. Gen. Robert L. Bullard, divisional commander from December 14, 1917 to July 14, 1918, is standing front row center. To Bullard's right is future Chief of Staff of the Army George C. Marshall. All of these men are wearing leather "Sam Browne" belts, which were worn by all Allied officers as a symbol of rank. Most of these officers have also pinned rank insignia to the front of their overseas caps. (SC6378)

Below: Officers of the 18th Infantry Regiment rest by the side of the road near Menil la Tour, France, in February 1918. Like their enlisted men, these officers are encumbered with a variety of equipment necessary for front-line service. The officer standing at right has pulled the flaps of his overseas cap down over his ears and placed his M1917 helmet on top. He has a khaki trench coat. Also of interest is the private purchase haversack worn on his left hip. (SC7590)

Above: Lieutenant Gillette, the chief of the 1st Division's photographic section, with his assistant, Sergeant Zimmerman. Gillette is wearing a winter parka and French-style overseas cap. He has pinned his rank insignia to the front of his cap. The sergeant is wearing the tight fitting M17 wool coat and breeches. Of interest are the rubber hip boots that he is wearing over his leggings and field boots. (SC6379)

Above right: Members of the 6th Field Artillery show off their improvised anti-aircraft gun at Menil la Tour. They have mounted a French Hotchkiss machine gun to a wagon wheel. The gun was issued to the 1st as a heavy machine gun. The gunner at right is loading a feeder strip of rounds into the gun. (SC7584)

Right: From left: Captain Logan, Lieutenant H.S. Young and Lt. J.G. Orlof from Company L, 16th Infantry, in February 1918. While Logan and Young are wearing private purchase officer's tunics with branch insignia and the U.S. national insignia, Orlof appears to be wearing a British-made enlisted man's tunic—distinguished by its rougher quality wool and internal pockets—with his civilian muffler. (SC7583)

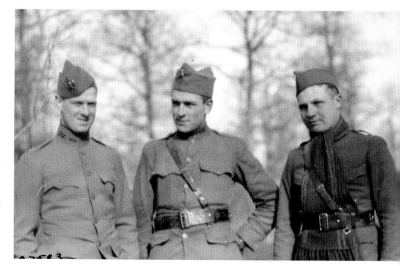

Above: An artilleryman from the 5th Field Artillery breaks into a grin after receiving refreshments and hot coffee from a Red Cross Canteen at Tour in March 1918. He is wearing an enlisted man's raincoat, which was made from rubberized canvas and closed with metal toggle buckles. A rubberized poncho later replaced it. (SC10430)

Above right: Secure in a revetted trench, a member of the 5th Artillery writes a letter home. Revetting a trench with woven branches was common among the French who taught the technique to the Americans. He is wearing a British dishpan helmet. The 1st received a great number of British helmets—distinguished by their smooth finish. (SC10441)

Right: A member of the 5th Field Artillery operates a Signal Corps M17 field telephone switchboard from a bunker at Menil la Tour in March 1918. From this switchboard, the battery commander could convey orders to each of his gun positions. (SC10346)

Left: Members of the 5th Field Artillery load their horses onto "40 and 8s." The "40 and 8" was the standard French railway car. On the outside of each car was painted a sign giving its capacity— 40 men or eight horses. The doughboys of the 1st division became well acquainted with these cars during the war. After the Armistice, one of the many veterans' organizations formed was the 40&8. (SC10437)

Left: Artillerymen from Battery E, 5th Field Artillery, load their French-manufactured 155mm Schneider Howitzers prior to a rail movement at Toul, France, in March 1918. There were 24 of the Schneiders in each U.S. Infantry Division. (SC10434)

Left: Red Cross volunteers give refreshments to members of the 5th Field Artillery at Toul. The 5th was one of the oldest artillery regiments in the Army and the division's heavy howitzer regiment. The Red Cross was one of the many civilian organizations that worked to support the welfare of the troops overseas. (SC10431)

Right: Officers from Company C, 26th Infantry Regiment, at Menil la Tour. These officers are wearing British box respirators on their left hips. The officer standing at left has obtained a cane to assist on the long road marches. He also has a pair of Type EE Bausch and Lomb field glasses in a leather case on his right hip. These glasses were marked U.S. Army Signal Corps. (SC10354)

Below: Major Theodore Roosevelt, the commander of the 1st Battalion, 26th Infantry Regiment, cites Lieutenant C.R. Holmes (left) and Sergeant Murphy, for bravery during a raid on German trenches near Bois l'Eveque in April 1918. Both of the officers wear private purchase leather trench boots. Roosevelt was the son of President Theodore Roosevelt and one of the 1st's legendary figures. He would later be awarded the Medal of Honor. (10360)

Left: Signalmen enjoy cigarettes provided by the Chicago Band Tobacco Fund. The free distribution of tobacco to doughboys at the front helped encourage widespread consumption of cigarettes in the United States after the war. Several of these men are holding their M1910 mess kits. These two-piece aluminum mess kits were stored in a mess kit carrier, which attached to the back of the pack. (SC13507)

Right: Major R.B. Paddock, the division signal officer for the 2nd Field Signal Battalion, poses for a picture at Mesnil St. Fermin. The major presents a fairly "regulation" appearance for an AEF officer. Officers were responsible for the purchase of their own clothing and generally bought items of a finer quality than enlisted uniforms. His overseas cap is adorned with his rank insignia and is piped in the Signal Corps' branch of service piping. (13503)

Left: Men from the division's 2nd Field Signal Battalion enjoy some letters from home while resting at Bonvillers, France, in May 1918. The soldier seated at left has obtained a pair of goggles to protect his eyes from dust. Rather than wear wool puttees, he wears a pair of leather leggings. His friend wears rubber hip boots over his field shoes. (SC13506)

Left: Members of the division's motorcycle dispatch service work on their bikes near Bonvillers. Many of the bikes used in the AEF were manufactured by Harley Davidson and were preferred over horses for delivering dispatches quickly. (SC13505)

Above: Sergeant F.D. Wolk from the 1st Division Dental Corps feeds his pet crow at Bonvillers. Wolk has a wristwatch on. Wristwatches first came into fashion during World War I and, like cigarettes, remained popular with doughboys once they returned to the United States. (SC13502)

Left: Members of the 28th Infantry Regiment fire on enemy positions near Bonvillers in May 1918. They are all using the .30-caliber M1903 Springfield rifles, which were standard issue to the 1st Division and widely regarded as the most accurate rifle in service in any army of that time. SC13501)

Left: Miss Ferguson and Miss Cornwall from American Red Cross Hospital Number 12 distribute chocolate and cigarettes to members of the 1st Engineers. Several of these men are wearing the olive drab 5-button wool flannel pull-over shirts that were standard issue to doughboys. (SC14697)

Right: Company A of the 1st Engineers marches down a road near Wirges, Germany, in December 1918. The company's guidon flag is between the two mounted officers at the head of the column. The flag had the Engineer Castle over the company designation. (SC34873)

Left: Members of the 1st Engineers disembark from a U.S.-designed "Liberty Truck" to enjoy a baseball game at Vermaise, France. The Liberty was developed with the assistance of leading U.S. vehicle manufacturers and was made of standardized interchangeable parts. Although these men are in a rear area, they all carry gas masks with them; a reminder that the war is not far away. (SC14695)

Lower left: Members of Company K, 16th Infantry Regiment, rest along a roadside near Coullemelle, France in June 1918. They are close enough to the front that most of these men continue to wear their helmets while working to clean their equipment. The man at right is in shirtsleeves and breeches, which illustrates their high waist. (SC14682)

Right: Sergeant S.L.B. Cohen of the 1st Machine Gun Battalion is waiting to be transported home after being wounded in June 1918. He is wearing wool tunic, breeches and overseas cap with cotton leggings. The gold V on his right sleeve signifies a wound; the one on his left denotes six months of overseas service. He has also been awarded the French *Croix de Guerre*, which is pinned over his left breast. (SC15077)

34873

15077

14920

Left: A gas alarm is sounded by a member of Company A, 1st Engineers, at Roncquecourt in June 1918. Gas was a constant threat and various means were devised to warn men when chemical agents were detected. This engineer is wearing his British box respirator at the ready position. The British mask can be identified by the leather tab on the right of the respirator case. (SC14920)

Left: Three officers in front of the division intelligence headquarters at the Verrier en Nesse Farm. These three men are wearing private purchase uniforms and leather trench boots. The officer standing at right has slipped on a brassard indicating his position on the division staff. (SC44278)

Below left: The citizens of Thelonne, France, thank a soldier from the 16th Infantry after their village's liberation. The soldier is wearing the full M1910 pack with tail. The canteen is attached to his ammunition belt and can be seen to the right of the tail. The individual first aid dressing pouch is to the left of the tail.

Bottom left: Weary and muddy, men of the 18th Infantry tramp through the Bois de Berlière. They present a typical front-line appearance. Of special interest is the man on the left who has obtained a French 2-liter canteen and has removed the sleeves from his enlisted raincoat. (SC44266)

Sentries from the 26th Infantry inspect a cart belonging to two German women at Hundsaugen, Germany. They are wearing the M1918 overcoat, which was a simplified version of the earlier overcoat, along with 10-pocket ammunition belts and canteens. (SC50763)

Above: Private E.A. Brotherhood talks to a French civilian in a recently liberated village. All of these doughboys are from the 16th Infantry. Brotherhood and his friends are wearing the M1910 web equipment over their enlisted overcoats. Brotherhood has attached his fearsome 18-inch bayonet to his Springfield 03 rifle. (SC44261)

Right: A Regular prior to crossing to France. This man is uniformed fairly typically of the doughboys before shipment to France. He is wearing wool shirt and trousers with campaign hat and canvas leggings. The canvas and leather scabbard for the 18-inch 03 bayonet can be seen on the right of the picture. Also visible is one of the pouches of his ammunition belt. This is an early model belt with eagle snaps on all the pockets rather than the lift-a-dot fasteners that would be found later.

Left: Staff officers gather outside headquarters. The one consistent feature of their uniforms is that they are all wearing leather Sam Browne belts, the universal Allied badge of rank for officers.

Above: A group of officers pose just behind the front line. The officer at left has a dispatch case resting on his right hip. The leather carrying case for a compass and the M1911 .45-caliber pistol can also be seen on his right side. Also of interest are the walking sticks that most of these men have obtained.

Left: A private from the 16th Infantry sits for a studio portrait. The bronze collar discs on his M1912 wool enlisted tunic are typical. The disc to the left is embossed with U.S., the one to the right has his regimental number (in this case 16) over crossed rifles (his branch of service) and his company designation. Later in the war, the branch of service disc would frequently be issued without regimental or company designations.

Right: "Lafayette we are here!" Members of the 1st Division parade through Paris after the division's arrival in France in June 1917. These men are all wearing campaign hats with canvas leggings and barracks shoes. Much of this early equipment would be replaced when it was found to be unsuited to the rigors of trench warfare.

Left: Doughboys from the 1st fire their Chauchat machine gun on German positions. Widely issued to American units, the Chauchat acquired an undeservedly poor reputation among many of the American soldiers.

Left: Enjoying the national pastime. Doughboys play a pickup game of baseball somewhere in France. The batter is wearing an issue white flannel undershirt. He has also removed his canvas leggings, which shows the cut of the issue breeches.

Left: A couple of doughboys fill their canteens from a Lister bag on a march in France. These men are both wearing the M1913 overcoat with the turn-back cuff. These coats were already out of date when the AEF shipped out for France, but older soldiers in Regular units like the 1st would have retained older garments.

Right: Assistant division commander, Brig. Gen. Terry de la Mesa Allen (center), confers with Marine General Holland Smith (left) and another officer during amphibious training maneuvers in North Carolina in August 1941. Both Army officers are wearing khaki cotton shirts and trousers with khaki cotton field hats. They are wearing their rank insignia on the epaulettes of their shirts. (SCS125101)

Right: Two mortarmen site their 81mm mortar during the New River, N.C., maneuvers. The man at left is wearing the blue denim fatigue uniform while the one on the right has received the newer green herring-bone twill (HBT) fatigue uniform. Both men are wearing World War I-vintage helmets and equipment. (SC125411)

Opposite page, top: 1st Division GIs return to their transports at the conclusion of maneuvers at New River. They are all wearing blue denim fatigues with khaki cotton field hats and M1910 equipment. They are hauling their heavy gear with hand pulled carts. (SC125045)

Opposite page, bottom: Troops enjoy a hot dinner in the field during the New River maneuvers. They are all wearing blue denim fatigues. Of special interest are the sergeant major's stripes being worn by the man at the head of the line. Generally, rank insignia was not worn on fatigue uniforms. (SC125161)

Below: A sergeant of the 1st Signal Company with his company's guidon. The flag is orange, for the Signal Corps, with the branch service insignia of crossed signal flags. Battle honors for the company's World War I campaigns are attached to the top of the flagpole. (SC138316)

Above: Officers of the 16th Infantry Regiment discuss the situation around Kasserine Pass. Three of these men have obtained winter combat jackets, which they are wearing over wool shirts and trousers. The three officers in shirtsleeves are wearing enlisted men's wool shirts. Officer's shirts had epaulettes and were often of finer material. (SC217387)

Below: Chaplain Bernard Henry leads members of the 1st Infantry Division in Easter services in North Africa. Warrant Officer W.W. Hughes, who plays a portable organ, is assisting Henry. All of these men are wearing the Parsons field jacket, which was named after Maj. Gen. James Parsons, the 3rd Corps Area commander who recommended its adoption. The jacket is better known as the M41 field jacket among collectors. (SC183822)

Left: A 2½ ton truck is unloaded from a British Landing Craft Assault (LCA) The LCA was the British version of the LCVP. Unlike the American-made assault craft, the British version featured armored curtains on the port and starboard sides.

Left: Curious 1st Division soldiers inspect a German rocket in Sicily. The man on the right has the divisional insignia displayed prominently on the front of his M1 helmet. Also of interest are the composition sole service shoes he is wearing. "Cap-toed" boots were worn stateside and once overseas were generally replaced by reverse upper "rough-out" service shoes. (SC180359)

Right: Italian prisoners are watched over by 1st Infantry Division personnel after their surrender at Nicosia, Sicily. The 1st Division men on the left are wearing first pattern HBT uniforms with leggings. The first pattern jackets were waist length and had a waistband. The trousers of the fatigue uniform lacked the thigh pockets of later versions. (SC185268)

Right: Members of the 1st Division provost detachment discuss how to care for Italian prisoners taken during operations in Sicily. Several of the men have military police (MP) brassards on their left sleeves. The brassard was made of dark blue wool with white wool lettering. The officer at the center has PM painted on his helmet for provost marshal, while several of his companions have the more common MP stencil on their helmets.

Right: Divisional Provost Marshal Major Thomas Lanser helps Sergeant William Cunningham prepare prisoner reports at Barafranca, Sicily, July 1943. Lanser has an early wool divisional patch on the left shoulder of his enlisted wool service shirt. He also appears to have obtained British web leggings that he is wearing in lieu of the taller U.S. leggings. (SC18461)

Left: After the victory in North Africa, division members of the 18th Infantry train at Port Aux Poules, Tunisia, for the Sicilian invasion. These men have landed from a Landing Craft, Infantry (LCI), another one of the workhorses of amphibious operations. An LCI could transport up to 188 fully equipped men ashore. This would allow a full company to land together on an invasion beach. (SC183982)

Below: Captain Edwin Elder from the 16th Infantry describes his short time as an Italian prisoner in Sicily. Elder's rank insignia (two silver bars) can be seen pinned to the right collar of his shirt. Although they are members of an infantry unit, several of the men in this picture have obtained tanker's jackets. (SC171633)

Above: Division commander Maj. Gen. Terry Allen (center) with his staff during the Sicilian campaign. He is wearing World War I era canvas leggings with his wool shirt and trousers. These officers have painted their rank insignia to the front of their helmets. Of interest is the large colonel's insignia painted on the helmet of the officer standing second from left. (SC424738)

Right: Frankie D'Alessandro, a member of the 18th Infantry, sits for a studio portrait on the division's return to England in preparation for the D-Day operation. Alessandro is wearing the wool service coat, which was constructed of 18-ounce olive drab wool serge. He is wearing the jacket with the wool shirt and khaki mohair tie. He has the branch of service and national insignia on his lapels but does not have any regimental distinctive insignia. (Gould collection)

Right: Dawn Gould of Weymouth celebrates her 17th birthday at the opening of the Red Cross club on January 30, 1944, with some of her friends from the 18th Infantry Regiment. All of the men are wearing the wool service jacket with khaki ties and wool shirts. None of these men have regimental distinctive insignia. The tie was supposed to be worn between the second and third button and not loose, as here. (Gould collection)

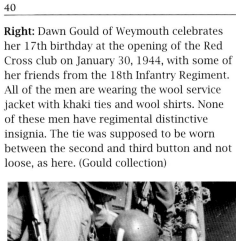

Left: Members of the 16th Infantry Regiment practice going down landing ladders into waiting LCVPs during training exercises at Slapton Sands a month prior to the invasion of France. The man standing on the left of the photograph with his back to the camera can be identified as an officer by the vertical white stripe painted on his helmet. Most of the men have bags for the M4 lightweight gas mask on their left hips. Although the masks were frequently discarded, the bags were often retained to carry additional personal possessions. (SC190096)

Right: Members of the 3rd Battalion, 16th Infantry Regiment, rest along the base of the cliffs overlooking Omaha Beach after their landing at Colleville-sur-Mer during the D-Day landing. The man standing with his back to the camera at left is wearing a canvas assault vest rather than the usual web equipment. Assault vests were specially designed one-piece vests that were worn by some members of the initial assault waves on D-Day. They were discarded after the invasion and not used again. (SC189932)

Right: The crew of an M1917A1 water-cooled .30-caliber Browning machine gun moves along Omaha Beach after the landing. The gunner is wearing an assault vest while his assistant has an ordinary M1928 pack. By 1944, the water-cooled Browning was being replaced by the M1919A4 air-cooled model.

Left: Members of the 1st Division wait to be taken to Omaha beach. The men in the foreground are wearing British-made mesh helmet nets. The sergeant in the center has a divisional insignia sewn to the left sleeve of his winter combat jacket. (SC190257)

Left: Lost members of the 1st on Omaha are led back to their units. The GI second from the left has an M1910 T-handle shovel clipped to the back of his assault vest. His bayonet (left of shovel) and canteen (right of shovel) can also be seen clipped to the vest. (SC189990)

Left: A medic of the 3rd Battalion, 16th Infantry Regiment, 1st Infantry Division, walks along Omaha Beach to treat wounded. He has scrim woven into his helmet net. The wider suspenders for supporting two medical pouches can be seen over his shoulders. He has slipped a Red Cross brassard over his left sleeve. (SC189925)

Above: PFC William Jackson and T/4 Joseph King enjoy improvised transportation after being relieved at Caumont, France, in July 1944 by the 5th Infantry Division. Both men are wearing wool trousers and shirts with field jackets. Jackson has an M1 carbine slung over his shoulder. (SC191565)

Above right: Private Joseph Richard sits by a gun position at Caumont prior to the division's relief. Richard is wearing a field jacket and an HBT uniform over his wool shirt and trousers. He has discarded his leggings, which gives a good view of the ankle-high service shoes. (SC191566)

Right: GIs from the 18th Infantry ride a tank into La Ferté-Macé, France, on August 14, 1944. Their appearance is typical of the men during the dash across France in the summer of 1944. The man at the left rear of the tank has an extra ammunition bag over his shoulder while the soldier next to him carries extra ammunition for his Garand rifle in a six-pocket cotton bandolier. (SC192706)

Above: Private Ginao Merli was credited with shooting 20 Germans during fighting in Belgium in September 1944, an achievement that would lead to the award of the Medal of Honor. Merli is wearing a field jacket over his wool uniform. As can be seen in this picture, the field jacket would quickly become soiled in combat. He has also woven canvas scrim into his helmet's net and buckled the chin strap around the back of the helmet. (SC193745)

Above right: Corporal A.L. Smith (left) and Private John Newcomber pick up rations for the 1st Signal Company at Kornelmunster, Germany. Smith is wearing an M1942 mackinaw Jacket. This blanket lined winter jacket was obsolete by 1944 but a severe shortage of adequate winter clothing led to older garments such as this being issued to the 1st and other units fighting in Europe. (SC204314)

Below: Members of the 1st Division prepare to receive decorations at the conclusion of the campaign through France. Most of these men are wearing field jackets with wool shirts and trousers. The white spot on the shoulders of some of the men was placed there for security reasons by a sensor to conceal the divisional insignia. (SC194887)

Right: Private Gene Pecorne (left) chats with T/4 Alva Pittman while Pittman's dog "Shickelgruber" looks out from a warm perch in December 1944. Percone has recently issued wool overcoats under his arm. These two men are both still wearing the field jackets that had been worn through the summer. The 1st Division does not appear to have started to receive large issues of the newer (and more versatile) M43 uniforms until early 1945. (SC197767)

Below: Division commander Maj. Gen. Clarence Huebner (left) with some recently decorated members of the 18th Infantry Regiment outside Aachen, Germany, which was the first German city seized by the Allies. These officers are wearing a variety of jackets including: Parsons field jackets, winter combat jackets and M1943 field jackets. Several of these men are wearing their combat infantry badges on their combat uniforms. (SC232964)

Above: A member of Company M, 18th Infantry Regiment, looks across a field near Sourbrodt, Belgium, during a search for misdropped German paratroopers at the start of the Ardennes Offensive in December 1944. He is still wearing a field jacket and trousers. The handle for his M43 folding shovel can be seen coming out from the back of his M1928 pack. The holster for a captured German P-38 pistol is on his right hip.

Below: Men of the 16th Infantry advance near Faymonville, Belgium, at the start of the Ardennes offensive. They have improvised snow camouflage from civilian sheets. The man at the left front of the column is also wearing white wool long underwear over his wool uniform. (SC198807)

Below: Infantrymen from the 26th Infantry Regiment move up to attack German forces near Büllingen, Belgium, at the start of the Ardennes offensive. The man at the front of the column has been fortunate enough to receive the new M43 cotton combat uniform. The new uniform was warmer and more rugged than the earlier field jacket. (SC198305)

Above: T/5 James King of the 1st Engineer Battalion inspects an American M8 armored car recaptured from the Germans in January 1945. King has obtained a pair of arctic overshoes. These shoes had rubber bottoms and canvas-treated uppers. He is also wearing an M1942 mackinaw jacket with divisional and rank insignia. (SC199163)

Top right: The crew of a 57mm anti-tank gun moves through Steinbach, Belgium, in January 1945. Each regiment had 18 of these guns to provide immediate firepower and anti-tank defense. The crew has improvised camouflage for their gun by draping the gunshield in a sheet. They have also fashioned white helmet covers from sheets. Although they were heavy and impractical, they are wearing their overcoats for additional warmth. (SC199184)

Above right: Men from the 1st Medical Battalion bring wounded division members to an improvised field hospital at Weywertz, Belgium, in January 1945. The medical personnel are wearing the Red Cross brassards on their left sleeve and their helmets have been painted with four red on white Red Crosses. (SC199211)

Right: 16th Infantry wounded are brought into a field hospital on the back of an M29 Weasel cargo carrier. The 5,400-pound M29 could carry up to 1,200 pounds of equipment. This small tracked vehicle was ideal for conditions in the Ardennes. (SC199213)

Left: Working in brutal conditions, GIs labor to free one of their 2½ ton trucks from the snow during the Ardennes fighting. The 2½-ton "deuce-and-a-half" was used in a tremendous variety of tasks. Each division had 356 listed in its table of organization and equipment. (SC199248)

Right: Soldiers listen attentively to instructions prior to moving out on a river crossing. They present a fairly typical appearance for 1st Division soldiers in early 1945, wearing a mixture of M1943 uniforms and earlier field jackets. The man at left has his M1 Garand slung over his right shoulder. The Army first adopted this .30-caliber weapon in 1936. An eight-shot semi-automatic rifle, it gave the ordinary American rifleman a tremendous firepower advantage over his opponents.

Left: A small treadway bridge is placed on the site of a destroyed stone bridge near Moderscheid, Belgium, during the Ardennes counteroffensive. The bridge is being lowered into place from the back of a "Bridge Erecting Truck." This 6-ton truck was manufactured by the Brockway Company and was specially designed to transport pre-manufactured bridge sections. (SC199463)

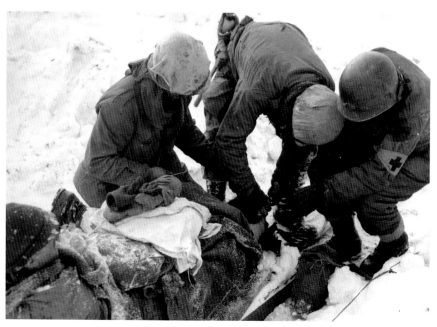

Left: An infantryman from the 26th Infantry Regiment wounded by a German mine in Büllingen, Belgium, receives medical treatment from three medics. A medical bag is resting at the feet of the man on the right. Each medic received two of these bags, which were issued with specially designed suspenders. (SC199652)

Right: PFC Sam Catericks reads graffiti on a building in Vetteweiss, Germany, in February 1945. Such messages were often scrawled on the sides of buildings in the final months of the war. Catericks has a woolen scarf tucked into the front of his field jacket for extra warmth. Local Red Cross chapters in the States often provided scarves, sweaters and other woolen items. (SC201529)

"Nur, wer mit geringen mittel Grosses tut, hat das Ziel richtig getroffen."

Above: "Blue Spaders" from the 26th Infantry Regiment wait in a shell crater for an artillery barrage to lift before moving on Soller, Germany, in February 1945. The squad's radioman is standing at the edge of the crater. His SCR-300/ BC 1000 man-pack radio is carried on his back. A BC 1000 was issued to each infantry platoon. (SC201690)

Left: The 18th Infantry Regiment's band performs for some infantrymen. The bandsmen are all wearing field jackets and trousers with rubber and canvas arctic overshoes. The band is complete with a portable piano. (SC201069)

Left: From left: PFC Phillip Graham, William Phillips and William Berthold examine a German aerial resupply container near Büllingen, Belgium. During the Battle of the Bulge, the 1st was involved in gathering up the remnants of a badly scattered German parachute drop. Graham has obtained a pair of trigger finger mittens. These mittens had a cotton poplin shell with a leather palm and a wool insert. (SC199689)

Right: A squad of men from Company I, 16th Infantry Regiment, ride through Schopen, Belgium, on the back of a Sherman tank in January 1945. A couple of these men are wearing snowsuits, which were manufactured in Belgium and began to reach front-line troops in very limited numbers toward the end of the Ardennes counteroffensive. Of special interest is the man seated in the center who wears a German snow parka. (SC248304)

Right: PFC Joseph Porecarelli of Company C, 18th Infantry Regiment, enjoys a newspaper during a rest period in the woods near Fusa, Germany, in February 1945. Porecarelli is wearing an issue high-neck sweater. Introduced with the M1943 uniforms, the high-neck sweater was wool and closed with five buttons. It had an elastic knit cuff and waistband that kept the sweater snug to the body. (SC201068)

Right: Rations for the 16th Infantry are unloaded from the back of a "deuce-and-a-half" at Fusa. The man at right wears a complete winter combat uniform, including jacket, wool lined bib-front overalls and wool lined cotton helmet. The zipper on the man's left leg allowed access to the pockets of trousers worn underneath. (SC200802)

Top left: Three men from Company F, 16th Infantry Regiment, keep a careful eye on Germans coming in to surrender at Weilerwist, Germany, in March 1945. The man on the right has rolled his trouser legs up over the top of his two-buckle combat boots. He has his M1943 folding entrenching tool attached to the left side of his belt. The folding shovel was modeled on a similar German shovel and replaced the earlier M1910 T-handle shovel. (SC248484)

Above: An NCO strides past two German civilians in Bleisheim, Germany, in March 1945. This GI has attached his bedroll around the bottom of the pack. This sort of improvisation was rather typical with the M1928 pack, which allowed the soldier to carry very little personal equipment. He also appears to have attached several grenades to his pack's meat-can pouch. (SC248482)

Center left: The ground crew of an L4 prepares their aircraft to take off for a mission from Alsdorf, Germany. Each infantry division was equipped with 10 of these lightweight aircraft. The unarmed L4s were used as artillery spotters and for reconnaissance work. (SC19259)

Left: The heavy weapons platoon of Company G, 18th Infantry, move out from their quarters at Weilerwist, Germany. The man fourth from the left has the 14-pound M2 tripod for his squad's M1919A4 .30-caliber machine gun. He has a .45-caliber pistol in its leather holster attached to the right side of his pistol belt. (SC248479)

Above: Sergeant Joe Phillips from Company D, 18th Infantry, fires an M1 2.36-inch rocket launcher. Popularly known as the "bazooka," the M1 used an electrical charge to launch a 2.36–inch M6 rocket at enemy targets out to 600 yards. Designed to provide an anti-tank capability to the infantry, three bazookas were issued to each weapons platoon. (SC24807)

Right: DUKW drivers warm themselves by a fire during the advance through Germany. The man seated at right is wearing the fiber liner for his M1 helmet. The liner could be quickly removed from the helmet shell and provide a lightweight head cover. Liners of 1st Division helmets were often painted with the division insignia. Later, more ornate decals were affixed to the shell. (SC248404)

Below: Captains Clement Van Wagoner, Jesse Miller and R.J. Linde from the 18th Infantry look over a divisional history pamphlet issued at the end of the war. The three men had the distinction of having served with the 1st since its landing in North Africa. Each of the gold bars on the left sleeves of their M43 field jackets represents six months' service overseas. They also have combat infantry badges pinned to their jackets, which was common in the 1st. (SC248381)

Left: A .30-caliber machine gunner prepares to move ahead. He has rested his 30lb weapon on his shoulder. A blanket is stowed in his M1928 pack. Additional personal items are carried in the canvas case for the M4 gas mask. Even though it is 1945 and the war in Europe is winding down, this man is equipped exactly as he would have been at Normandy more than a year before. (SC248422)

Opposite page, bottom: Infantrymen in Gladbach, Germany, wait beside M10 Tank Destroyers of the 634th Tank Destroyer Battalion. Not officially part of the division, the 634th was assigned to support the 1st from August 1944 to May 1945. Other tank destroyer and tank battalions were attached to the division at various times. (SC248462)

Right: PFC Joseph Pichierre from the 18th Infantry Regiment guards the cell of Nazi Rudolf Hess during the Nuremberg war crimes trial. Pichierre is wearing an M1939 Wool Service Coat with wool trousers, M1 helmet liner and well-polished two-buckle boots. His coat has the divisional and rank insignia on the right sleeve. The *fourragère*, a regimental distinction awarded by the French government during World War I, is worn around the left shoulder. Pichierre's DIs can be seen on the lapels of his jacket. (SC220076)

Below: Belgian Defense Minister Leon Mundelear attaches the *fourragère* of the Belgian *Croix de Guerre* to the division's colors. The *fourragère* represented the second award of the *Croix de Guerre* to the division during World War II. The 1st also received two *Croix de Guerres* from the French government. The color guard are wearing M1942 enlisted wool overcoats, M1 helmet liners and 2-buckle boots. (SC220061)

Left: Assistant division commander Brig. Gen. George Taylor accepts the surrender of Lt. Gen. Fritz Benicke at Elbogen, Germany, on May 7, 1945. Taylor and his translator, Captain Carl Oelve, are both wearing winter combat jackets. Oelve has an M1911A1 .45 pistol in an M3 shoulder holster. His divisional insignia has been sewn to the left sleeve of his jacket. (SC206599)

Left: Maj. Gen. Walter Robertson (right) presents the Medal of Honor to Staff Sergeant Joseph E. Schaefer. Schaefer was one of the division's 16 Medal of Honor recipients during World War II. He has a 1st Division decal attached to the front of his M1 helmet liner and is wearing the wool field jacket, popularly known as the "Ike" jacket. Originally intended as a liner to the M1943 field jacket, by the end of the war the Ike had come to be most frequently used as a dress garment.

Right: Sergeant Ronald Myers leads a tank into Riefenbeek, Germany, in April 1945. The censor has removed the divisional insignia from the jackets of the men in the photo. Myers is wearing an M1943 field jacket and HBT fatigue trousers. Around his waist is an M1923 ammunition belt in the dark OD7 shade, which began to reach the front late in 1944. (SC206362)

Below: An officer (left) addresses his men in Mittelscheid, Germany, in March 1945. The men on the left and the right of the first row are wearing arctic field jackets, which were similar to the regular field jacket but lined with a blanket-weight material and longer in the waist. The GI in the center is wearing an M43 jacket. It is interesting to note that the officer is wearing nothing that would indicate his rank. Under combat conditions officers would endeavor to be as inconspicuous as possible. (SC374834)

Left: Men from the 18th Infantry enjoy the enlisted club in Eibsee, Germany, in January 1946 while waiting to be shipped home. In the relaxed atmosphere of the club these soldiers are allowed to wear a variety of wool uniforms and HBT fatigue clothing. The woman serving second from the left is an official Army hostess. (SC226771)

Left: A 1st Division vehicle crew enjoys some music during a break in Exercise Shamrock, a training exercise in Germany in March 1950. They are wearing a variety of World War II-era equipment including pile field caps, M43 jackets and 2-buckle combat boots. The enormous amount of material produced for the war meant that World War II items would continue to be used well into the 1950s. (SC353741)

Left: The divisional colors pass in review during a ceremony at Darmstadt, Germany, in August 1951. The color guard members are all wearing M1 helmets that have been nickel treated for dress occasions, with white web belts and cross straps. The white laces of their jump boots have been made from parachute shroud lines. (SC384374)

Right: Captain Harold Bartlett (left) explains the history of the division to Captain Stanley Spratt, a visiting British officer. Bartlett is wearing an officer's quality Ike jacket with trousers and overseas cap. All of these uniform components were made in olive drab shade 51 fabric similar to the officer's uniforms worn during World War II. He is wearing this uniform with a poplin khaki shirt and dark tie. In addition to his rank insignia, his overseas cap is piped in the black and gold braid universal to all officer ranks below general. (460555)

Below: An honor guard fires a salute during a ceremony at the Colleville-sur-Mer cemetery overlooking Omaha Beach on the 10th anniversary of the D-Day landings. The cemetery is the resting place for more than 9,000 American servicemen, many of them from the 1st Division, killed in France during World War II. The men of the firing party are wearing the M1950 OD jacket and trousers in olive drab shade 33 wool serge. The M1950 jacket was a more refined version of the World War II era jacket. (SC527191)

Below: World War I veterans visit the 16th Infantry Regiment during a field problem in the early 1960s. The two officers are wearing olive green (OG) 107 cotton sateen utility uniforms with "blocked" caps and black jump boots. In 1952 the cotton sateen utility uniform replaced the HBT clothing that had been worn since World War II. The officer at right has a regimental crest sewn to his left breast pocket. (SC498574)

Left: Brigadier General John Seitz, Maj. Gen. Harvey Fischer and Brig. Gen. William Kunzig stand behind a plaque bearing the divisional motto during ceremonies in June 1960 to mark the 42nd anniversary of the founding of the division. The three officers are wearing well-pressed khaki cotton uniforms. The three also have green combat leader tabs on their shirt epaulettes. (SC585170)

Left: Two members of the 1st enjoy a last cup of coffee before leaving Fort Riley, Kansas, en route to South Vietnam. Both men are wearing OG107 utility uniforms with full color insignia. Each has a white nametape over the right breast and the black and gold U.S. Army tab over the right. A regimental badge is sewn to the left breast pocket. (SC623420)

Left: 1st Division soldiers board a passenger train at Fort Riley at the start of the trip to South Vietnam in November 1965. All of these men are wearing OG107 cotton utility uniforms with M1951 field coats. After the men arrived in the tropical heat of Vietnam, the field coats were quickly discarded. (SC625338)

Above: Captain J.F. Fletcher, the commander of Company C, 28th Infantry Regiment, "The Lions of Cantigny," issues final orders prior to moving into contact with the enemy during operations in November 1965. Fletcher is talking into the handset of his AN/PRC-10 radio. (SC635759)

Above right: An armored personnel carrier of Company C, 28th Infantry Regiment, halts on a road leading to the Midule rubber plantation during operations in November 1965. The GI in the foreground has a sock full of personal items tied to the left strap of his M1956 LBE (Load Bearing Equipment). He has clipped a flashlight to the right side of his harness. Although more versatile than earlier equipment sets, soldiers still improvised how they set up their M1956 LBE. (SC635758)

Right: Troopers wait for UH-1D "Huey" Helicopters to transport them to the battle area. They are equipped with the 7.62mm M14 rifle, which replaced the M1 Garand. Although production of the M14 had ceased in 1964 when the Army began preparing to manufacture the M16, most of the early units shipped to Vietnam, including the 1st, were initially equipped with the M14. (SC635347)

Above: Armored personnel carriers from the 4th Cavalry Regiment move along Highway 13, "Thunder Road," during a road clearing operation. The 4th was part of the division's reconnaissance element. The vehicle commander is wearing a Combat Vehicle Crewman's (CVC) helmet and M1952 flak vest. (635342)

Above right: Members of Company C, 28th Infantry, stand ready to move into a rubber plantation north of Saigon in November 1965. These three men have extra belts of linked ammunition for their squad's 7.62mm M60 machine gun. Each belt held 100 rounds of ammunition. As the belt was fed into the machine gun it would disintegrate. (SC624682)

Left: Chief of Staff of the Army Gen. Harold Johnson visits Battery C, 2nd Howitzer Battalion, 35th Artillery, at Xuan Loc. The small canisters hanging from the belt loops of the crew are for earplugs, which were helpful when firing the massive 155mm howitzer, they are standing in front of. (SC635064)

Right: After exiting their UH-1D Huey helicopters at Ben Dong So members of the 1st Division quickly clear the landing zone (LZ). These men are traveling light but even so the ones in the foreground have each clipped two full plastic one-quart canteens to their individual equipment belts. (SC624622)

Right: Two members of the 1st man a .50-caliber machine gun position at Ben Dong So in October 1965. Despite its weight, the 82-pound HB (Heavy Barrel) M2 .50-caliber Browning machine gun was used extensively in Vietnam. The World War II-era weapon could fire 450–575 rounds of .50-caliber ammunition per minute. (National Archives)

Right: An OH-13 Sioux helicopter sets down in a 1st Division LZ. The Sioux was used, much like the light spotter planes employed during World War II, for observation and target acquisition. Having first entered service in 1956, the Sioux was replaced by the OH-64 Cayuse by 1966. (National Archives)

Left: A 105mm howitzer from the 1st Battalion, 7th Artillery, fires on enemy positions in the Rung Sat special zone during Operation Charleston in December 1966. This gun has been fixed to a Landing Craft, Mechanized (LCM), in order to bring it closer to the enemy. The M102 could hit targets out to a range of 8½ miles. Each of the division's four artillery battalions had 24 of these guns. (636330)

Below left: Army Chief of Staff Gen. Johnson speaks to the men of the 1st Battalion, 26th Infantry, in August 1966. The soldiers behind the podium are all wearing the first pattern tropical combat uniform, better known as the jungle uniform. The officer in the foreground has a black leather M1 holster for a .45-caliber pistol fixed to his equipment belt. Other than color, the holster was little changed from that first issued during World War I. (SC635063)

Below right: Soldiers from Company C, 18th Infantry, slosh through the swamps of the Rung Sat Special Zone during Operation Lexington. These two tired men are wearing OG107 utility uniforms with utility caps. The caps have the 18th Infantry Regimental DI pinned to the front. As can be seen in this picture, the utility cap became badly misshapen during operations in the heat of Vietnam. (SC633636)

Right: Two members of the 18th in the Rung Sat Special Zone. The man at the front is wearing a first pattern tropical combat jacket (with exposed buttons) and the hated utility cap. He is wearing a privately acquired medal on his dog tag chain, which can be seen around his neck. (SC633635)

Below: Weary members of the 1st Division board a waiting LCM that will take them to a rest camp at the end of Operation Lexington in September 1966. These soldiers are wearing a mixture of OG107 utility and tropical combat uniforms that were typical of that period of the war, when improved uniforms and equipment more suited to the conditions in Vietnam began to reach the soldiers in greater numbers. (National Archives)

Left: 1st Division troopers unload from their LCM at the end of Operation Lexington. Some of these men have slipped bottles of insect repellent into the elastic camouflage helmet band. In the center of the group is a soldier wearing a locally manufactured bush hat. (National Archives)

Left: Men unload from their LCM at the end of Operation Lexington. As was customary, several of them have M26A1 fragmentation grenades clipped to the sides of their M1956 universal pouches. The pouches had special retaining straps that allowed the grenades to be safely carried. (National Archives)

Left: Engineers patrol a river in the Iron Triangle on a specially devised gun platform. The "raft" carries a World War II-era M45 anti-aircraft mount and at least one M60 machine gun mounted on a platform that rested on two RB15 rubber boats. The M45 housed four .50-caliber machine guns in a rotating mount. (SC624247)

Above left: A soldier from the 2nd Infantry runs toward the jungle at Phuoc Vinh in 1967. This man is wearing his unit's distinctive black scarf. The use of colored scarves was not uncommon and was inspired by scarves originally worn by members of the South Vietnamese Army. (SC642376)

Above right: With his helmet covered in foliage, a soldier of the 2nd Battalion, 28th Infantry, gets ready to move forward during Operation Billings. He has secured all of the foliage underneath the elastic camouflage helmet band. He has a set of locally manufactured black velvet subdued sergeant's stripes on the sleeves of his jungle jacket. (SC640452)

Below: Grunts from the 2nd Battalion, 28th Infantry, move through tall grass during Operation Billings. The distinctive tape antenna of the AN/PRC-25 radio can clearly be seen on the back of this unit's RTO. (SC640453)

Left: A machine-gun team from Company C, 16th Infantry Regiment, rises up from their protective cover with their M60. The assistant gunner helps carry the 100-round belt of ammunition to prevent it from twisting or getting dirty as they advance. (SCC32309)

Opposite page, top: President Richard M. Nixon visits with members of the 1st Division at Di Ann. All of these men are wearing the third pattern cotton poplin tropical combat uniform with subdued insignia and nametapes. The tapes are worn parallel with the ground, which dates this photograph to some time after October 1969. Prior to that, the tapes were worn parallel to the edges of the pocket flap. The third pattern of this highly regarded uniform featured concealed buttons and did away with the earlier shoulder epaulettes. (SC652436)

Left: Members of the 28th Infantry wait to board their UH-1Ds during Operation Billings. These men have liberally festooned themselves with foliage. The soldier on the right has even hung branches from the back of his lightweight rucksack. He has also filled the thigh pockets on his jungle trousers. These trousers featured a bellows pocket on each thigh. (SC640448)

Left: SP4 Mack, a "tunnel rat" in Company B, 26th Infantry, prepares to enter a North Vietnamese tunnel complex during Operation Cedar Falls in January 1967. He is wearing the second pattern of the cotton poplin jungle jacket with shoulder epaulettes and concealed pocket buttons. He has several P-38 can openers stuffed behind his camouflage helmet band. The P-38 came with the C-rations and was used to open up the ration's canned components. (SC637880)

Right: SP4 Jack Brinsonn of the 28th Infantry lays down a base of fire during a battle at Thu Duc in 1968. Brinson is wearing a tropical combat uniform. He has two assistants with spare belts of 7.62mm ammunition nearby. (SC646258)

Above: A member of Company A, 26th Infantry, rests by a tree before moving ahead during an operation in 1967. He is armed with an M16A1 rifle, which was the most widely used U.S. infantry weapon of the Vietnam War. At 8.4 pounds, the rifle was half the weight of the earlier M14 rifle. It was a selective-fire weapon that could be fired either on semi-automatic or full automatic. Each magazine carried 20 rounds of 5.56mm ammunition. This man has the earlier three-pronged flash suppressor on the end of the rifle. (SC36330)

Above: A Big Red One soldier watches the bushes during a resupply convoy on Highway 16 in January 1967. He is wearing M1952 "flak vest" body armor. Generally, Army personnel dispensed with flak vests, which were hot and uncomfortable. He is armed with a 40mm M79 grenade launcher, known to the Grunts as the "thumper." The M79 was a hand-held weapon that could fire high explosive or smoke rounds to over 400 yards. (SC636327)

Left: Members of the 2nd Battalion, 28th Infantry, clear an LZ during Operation Billings. Each of the hovering UH-1D Huey helicopters could bring 11 fully armed GIs into the landing area. (SAA2333)